ACCOUNTANCY

PART-1

:: Author ::

ROBIN N. VORA

(M.COM., B.ED., SLET)
GUJARAT UNIVERSITY RANKER

PUBLISHED BY

The New Era International Publishing House
HQ. At & Po. Chaveli., Ta- Chansma,
Dist- Patan, North Gujarat, India, Asia.

First Publication: 1st FEBRUARY, 2015

Copyright: Author
(c) ROBIN N. VORA

ISBN:- 978-15-08472-66-7

Price: Rs.750/- INDIA
        $ 15 OUTSIDE INDIA

PUBLISHED BY

The New Era International Publishing House
HQ. At & Po. Chaveli., Ta- Chansma,
Dist- Patan, North Gujarat, India, Asia.

Dedicated to my Parents

INDEX

CHAPTER – 1

"Introduction to Accounting and Explanation of Accounting Terms"

☐ THEORY SECTION ☐

⇒ In ancient times accounts were maintained in ancient China, Egypt, Greek and Italian culture.

⇒ The **Italian Monk Luka Pacioli** for the first time in **1494 A.D.,** in his book on Mathematics, made presentation of the currently in use double entry accounting system.

⇒ **According to AICPA** (American Institute of Certified Public Accounts) :

" Accounting is the process of recording, classifying, analyzing and interpreting the business transactions which can be measured in terms of money in such a way that it helps users in taking correct decisions."

⇒ **Objectives of Accounting :**

✓ To keep the record of every business transaction which takes place during the specified period.

✓ To know the true financial position of the business after determining the effect of all transactions during the accounting period.

✓ To evaluate the profitability or earning capacity of the business.

✓ To provide useful information to know the efficiency of the manager.

✓ To provide useful information to government for taking proper decisions about taxes.

✓ It can be produced as a legal evidence in future.

✓ To provide necessary information for preparing budget and also control can be exercised over various activities of the business.

⇒ **<u>Advantages of Accounting</u> :**

❖ By maintaining accounts, the owner of the business can get any accounting information whenever required.

❖ From the business activities, profit or loss can be known at the end of the year.

❖ From the prepare final accounts, financial position can be known at the end of the year.

❖ Books of accounts can be produced as a legal evidence.

❖ With the help of accounting thefts, frauds, manipulations, malpractices etc. can be found out and controlled.

❖ Accounting provide necessary information for decision making.

❖ Current year's information can be compared with the information of the previous year and with that of other firms.

❖ Accounting information is necessary to determine the taxes payable to the government.

❖ Bank, creditors, shareholders, employees, government etc. can obtain information regarding their interest.

⇒ **<u>Limitations of Accounting</u> :**

➢ Non financial transactions are not recorded in the books of accounts though it has its own importance.

➢ Financial transactions are measured only in terms of money.

➢ Many times, accounting information is based on estimates.

Example, discount reserve on debtors, closing value of stock etc. These estimates can be incorrect.

➢ Sometimes it does not show real position.

Example, fixed assets are shown at cost price less depreciation, but if its market value is different, it is not considered.

➢ Sometimes actual position is not reflected due to personal bias of the accountant.

Example, estimating the loss like bad debts, bad debts reserve.

⇒ **Qualitative Characteristics of Accounting Information**

- **Understandability :** Accounting information should be presented in a clear and proper form with necessary information, so that the users of the information can be clearly understand it, which is nothing but the main objective of accounting.

   Ex. If an accounting statement is prepared with improper language, improper classification of the particulars etc.

- **Relevance_:** The books of accounts prepared by the business unit should be prepared by in such a way that the objective of writing the books of accounts should be fulfilled and relevant information should be provided in that context. Ex. The person who is giving the loan would require to know whether the assets are free of charge? Whether they are recorded at the proper value?

- **Reliability :** Accounting information should be reliable. The reliability of accounts depends upon the honesty of the accountant.

- **Comparability :** Accounting information should have the quality of comparability. With this accounting information of the same firm can be comparable for the different years. Most of the company provides the figures of the current years with the figures of the previous years, in their annual report, just for the comparison purpose only.

⇒ **Basic Accounting Terms :**

♣ **Business Transactions :** "Transactions means exchange between two or more persons or firms. If such exchange can be measured in terms of money, then only it is known as business transaction." Business transactions affected financial position of the business.

In other words, any exchange of goods or services, against money is known as business transaction. There are two types of economic transactions:

1) **Cash transactions :** which includes exchange of cash and transaction entered into through banks.

2) **Credit transactions :** In which the payment of cash is deferred for some time.

♣ **Debit :** To debit means recording an amount on the debit side (left hand side) of a ledger account. The name of account credited should be written in the column of particulars.

♣ **Credit :** To credit means recording an amount on the credit side (right hand side) of a ledger account. The name of account debited should be written in the column of particulars.

♣ **Capital (credit) :** "When cash, goods, or assets brought by the owner in the business is known as capital." In other words, capital means excess of business assets over liabilities.

Formula : Capital (net assets or net worth) = Total assets – Total liabilities

♣ **Drawings (debit) :** "When cash, goods, or assets withdrawn by the owner in the business is known as drawings." Due to drawings decrease in capital.

♣ **Liability (credit) :** "Any amount payable by the business to any outsiders is known as liability." It can be created by credit purchase of goods and also by borrowing funds.

There are two types of liabilities.

1. **Current liability :** Amount payable within **1** year is called current liability.

2. **Long term liability :** Amount payable after **1** year is called long term liability.

♣ **Assets :** "Items having realizable value owned by the business are known as assets and assets owned by the business are known as business assets."

Assets are classified mainly into three types.

1) **Fixed assets :** The assets which can be used for a long period in the business are known as immovable or fixed assets.

Example, land, building, goodwill, furniture ,patent etc.

2) **Current assets :** The form of which are changing frequently with the transactions of the business are known as current assets.

Example, cash, bank balance, stock, tools, etc.

3) **Fictitious assets :** Certain expenses, the benefit of which is available for more than one year, are not written off in one year but are shown as fictitious assets on the assets side of the balance sheet.

Example, preliminary expenses, discount on debentures, discount on shares,

advertisement campaign expenses.

✓ **Other classification of assets is** :

1. **Tangible assets :** Those assets which can be seen, touch are known as tangible assets.

Example, land, building, vehicles, furniture, patent etc.

2. **Intangible assets :** Those assets which cannot be seen, touch are known as intangible assets.

Example, goodwill, patent, trademark, copyright.

♣ **Purchase (debit) :** " The items in which the trader is trading are called goods."

Goods received by the trader for cash on credit are known as purchase.

♣ **Sales (credit) :** " Goods given by the trader for cash on credit to the customers as known as sales."

♣ **Debtors (debit) :** When the goods or services are sold to the customers on credit and the total amount receivable from customers is known as receivables. All such customers are known as debtors of the business.

♣ **Creditors (credit) :** The total amount payable to the persons supplying goods or providing services on credit is known as debt. Such persons are known as creditors of the business.

♣ **Bad debts (debit) :** The amount which is to be forgone, totally or partly, out of the total receivable amount from a debtor, is known as bad debts or irrecoverable amount. Bad debts is always one kind of loss for the business.

♣ **Bad debts recovered (credit) :** The amount which was forgone as bad debts, when paid by the debtor. Due to improvement of financial position is known as bad debts recovered. Bad debts recovered is always income for the business.

♣ **Stock (debit) :** At the end of the accounting year, the stock of the goods unsold or unutilized is known as closing stock for the current year. It would be considered as the opening stock for the next accounting year.

♣ **Revenue (credit) :** Amount received or receivable, for the goods or services sold to the customers and incomes like interest, discount, commission etc. are known as revenue.

♣ **Expense (debit) :** There are two types of expenses:

♥ **Revenue expenses :** If the benefit of the amount spent is available to the business for the accounting year only, then it is known as revenue expenses.

♥ **Pre paid expenses :** If the benefit is available to the business for more than one year, then the amount spent for the future period is known as pre paid expenses.

Ex., rent paid in advance

♣ **Expenditure (debit) :** Amount spent or paid or when the liability is created for getting any benefit or service is known as expenditure.

Ex., purchase of furniture, payment of salary.

♣ **Income (credit) :** Amount received on sale of goods or services or business assets is known as income. There are two types of incomes:

♠ **Revenue income :** Income received from the day to day transactions of the business

is known as revenue income.

Ex., interest received, discount received, commission received etc.

♠ **Capital income :** Income received on sale of any assets or on receipt of any long term

debt is known as capital income.

Ex., income from sale of machinery, amount received on issue of shares.

♣ **Receivables :** Amount receivable from any person other than the debtors, pre-paid expenses, from customers is known as receivables. All such customers are known as debtors of the business.

♣ **Payables :** Amount payable to any person other than the creditors, outstanding expenses, income received in advance, are known as payables.

♣ **Profit (Gain- credit) :** Gain means profit made as a result of business transactions. In other words, during the year, if revenue incomes are more than revenue expenses as a result of business transactions, it is known as profit or gain. Owner's capital increases due to profit.

♣ **Loss (debit) :** Loss means amount loss without getting any benefit. In other words, during the year, if revenue expenses are more than revenue incomes as a result of business transactions, it is known as loss. Owner's capital decreases due to loss.

⇒ **Method or Systems of Accounting :**

There are mainly **two types** of accounting :

✓ **Double Entry Accounting System** : In this method, in book – keeping, each transaction is given two effects

(i) debit effect (ii) credit effect. The amount debited is equal to the amount credit. This method was first time represented by Italian Monk Luca Pacioli and it is most important, more scientific and widely used method in many countries of the world including India of accounting.

✓ **Deshi Nama Accounting System** : Deshi Nama Accounting System of book – keeping is the oldest method of writing the books of accounts in India. This method of accounting is very easy and simple. This system differs structurally from double entry system though the principles are the same in both methods. This system is also known as ' **Bahi khata**' system.Two main books are maintained under this method :

1. **Rojmel**, which satisfies the requirements of cash book and journal.

2. **Khatavahi**

…………×××××××××………

CHAPTER – 2

"Two – Fold Effects of Transaction"

☐ THEORY SECTION ☐

❖ **There are two types of transactions :**

1. **Economic transaction** : Those business transactions which can be measured in terms of money or where receipt or payment of money is involved are known as economic transaction.

   E.g. Palav sold furniture of **Rs. 15,000.**

2. **Non – economic transaction** : Those business transactions which cannot be measured in terms of money or where receipt or payment of money is involved are known as economic transaction.

❖ **Types of Economic transactions:**

✓ **Cash transaction**

a) Assets Transaction

b) Goods Transaction

c) Services Transaction

d) Debt Transaction

✓ **Transaction for goods or services**

a) Services Transaction

b) Assets Transaction

✓ **Transactions Involving Receivables & Payable**

❖ **Accounting Transactions :**

There are mainly three types of parts :

1) **Cash transaction :** A transaction wherein cash comes in or goes out from the business or a transaction entered

through banks is known as cash transaction. Because of cash transactions, cash or bank balance increases or decreases.

E.g., Sold goods for **Rs. 5,000.**

2) **Credit transaction :** A transaction in which the payment of cash is deferred for some time, then it is known as credit transaction. A relation of debtor – creditor take place, because of credit transaction.

E.g., Purchased goods of **Rs. 1,500** from Jay.

3) **Other special transactions :** Transactions like the following which are neither cash nor credit are required to be recorded in the books of account as they are real transactions.

E.g. goods destroyed by fire, goods distributed as free samples.

❖ **Rules of Cash or Credit transaction :**
✓ If the given transaction specifically mentions it to be on cash or cheque – **Cash transaction.**

E.g. – Purchased goods of **Rs. 500** by cheque.
✓ In a given transaction, if the name of the person is given and also information relating to cash or cheque is given then – **Cash transaction.**

E.g. Sold goods worth of **Rs. 1,800** to Harshil for cash.
✓ In a given transaction, if the name of the person is given but information relating to cash or cheque is not given. – **Credit transaction.**

E.g. Sold goods worth of **Rs. 1,800** to Jayshil.

✓   If the given transaction does not mention the name of the person and also does not specify it to be on cash or cheque. - **Cash transaction.**

E.g. – Purchased machinery of **Rs. 25,000.**

✓   If the given transaction specifically mentions words like paid, received, deposited - **Cash transaction.**

E.g. Paid salary of **Rs. 4,000** to Nirav.

❖ **Accounting Equation (A = C + L) :** Under double entry book-keeping system, sum of liabilities and capital is always equal to assets. This can be represented as under in the form of an equation.

     If Assets is denoted by 'A', Liabilities by 'L' and Capital by 'C', the equation can be as under. **A = C + L OR A = L + C**

     Under double entry system of book- keeping, every business transaction has two-fold effect and dual aspect of each transaction affects changes in assets, liabilities and capital in such a manner that the basic accounting equation is satisfied. If we examine two – fold effect of any transaction, it results into increases or decreases in assets and/or in liability or capital.

     This accounting equation is also known as Balance Sheet Equation. Mathematically the following equation can be made from this :

C = A – L.........(1)

L = A – C.........(2)

In **(1)** equation above, the net/residual amount remaining after deducting liabilities from assets is known as net capital of business. However equation **(2)** is not true because C is a residual value.

E.g. ♠ Gave a cheque of **Rs. 5,500** to Binal towards amount payable.

Effects : (a) Binal receives → Liability decreases

(b) Amount paid by cheque → Bank balance decreases

[A and L have decreases by same amount.]

❖ **Difference between Cash and Credit transaction :**

No.	Points	Cash Transaction	Credit Transaction
1	**Definition**	A transaction wherein cash comes in or goes out from the business or a transaction entered through banks is known as cash transaction.	A transaction in which the payment of cash is deferred for some time, then it is known as credit transaction.
2	**In Information in Transaction**	In such transaction specifies that it is for cash OR there is no mention about cash or name of person.	In such transaction, there is only name of person without specifying that it is for cash.
3	**Exchange**	Mainly cash or cheque is exchanged	Cash or cheque is not exchanged in

		in a Cash transaction.	a Credit transaction.
4	**Effect on Account**	In such transaction, one account affected is that of cash or bank. Thus, cash or bank balance increases or decreases.	In such transaction, one account affected is of person. The person is either receiver or giver.
5	**Relation**	No any relation takes place because of Cash transaction.	A relation of debtor-creditor tales place because of Credit transaction.
6	**Entry**	Such transactions are recorded in Cash Book.	Such transactions are recorded in Purchase Book, Sales Book, Returns Book, or in Journal.

❖ **Voucher :**

"Voucher is an evidence supporting the transaction recorded in books of accounts." Since such evidence is in the written form, it could be preserved for a very long time.

⇒ E.g. cash memo, bills, pay-in-slip.

⇒ This can be explained with the help of the following table.

E.g. the following vouchers recording in books of accounts of A.(Owner of the Business)

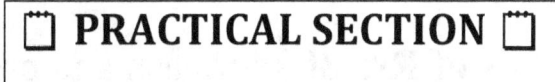

⌐ PRACTICAL SECTION ⌐

1. **Explain Two – fold effects of the following transactions with the help of accounting equation .**
   ✓ Tal started a business by bringing cash of **Rs. 15,000.**
   ✓ Paid bank charges of **Rs. 100.**
   ✓ Sold furniture for **Rs. 3,000.**
   ✓ Purchased goods of **Rs. 6,500** from Arpanbhai.
   ✓ Appointed Harshil as accountant at a salary of **Rs. 11,000** per month.
   ✓ Returned goods of **Rs. 4,000** to Jay.

2. How the dual effects of the following transactions with the help of accounting equation.

   ✓ Ashish started his business with cash **Rs. 35,000.**

   ✓ Life insurance premium paid **Rs. 2,500** by cash.

   ✓ Purchased Narmada Nigam Bond for **Rs. 2,700.**

   ✓ Received commission **Rs. 700.**

✓   Opened a bank account by depositing **Rs. 10,000** cash.

✓   Paid income tax **Rs. 1,020** by cheque.

✓   Purchased furniture of **Rs. 8,500** from Harshalbhai.

✓   Decide to give advance salary of **Rs. 4,000** to manager.

3.   State how will you interpret the following vouchers in the books of accounts of Nikhil .

❖   Sold goods of **Rs. 300** for cash and prepare cash memo for it.

❖   Goods of **Rs. 5,000** purchased from Naimesh. He sent cash memo along with it.

❖   Nikhil issued a debit note of **Rs. 200** to Bhavya.

…………×××××××××………

CHAPTER -3

"TYPES OF ACCOUNTS"

☐ THEORY SECTION ☐

❖ **Definition of Account :**

When transactions affecting a particular aspect/matter are recorded properly at on place and a summary is drawn, that is known as an account thus, every account is divided into two parts. The left hand side is known as the **"Debit side"** and the right hand side as the **"Credit side"**

⇒ **There are mainly two types of accounts :**

(1) Personal Accounts

(2) Impersonal Account : There are two types of impersonal account.

♣ Real Accounts

♣ Nominal Account

✓ **Personal Accounts :-** Credit transactions in a business are carried out with a living person, an institution or an artificial person. As a result of such credit transactions, debtor-creditor (receiver or giver) relationship arises.

   E.g. Gujarat electric Board's account, Ahmedabad Education Society's account.

✓ **Real Accounts :-** The product traded in a business is known as goods separate accounts are maintained for incoming and outgoing of Goods.

The real accounts of a business can be classified into two groups :

(1) Goods Accounts

(2) Assets Accounts

❖ **Goods Accounts :-** Generally, the following accounts arise as a result of the transactions relating to the exchange of goods :

E.g. Purchase Account, Sales Account, Purchase Return Account, Sales Return Account etc.

❖ **Assets Accounts :-** An item or a right owned by the business and having financial value is known as an asset. Such assets are useful for the proper running of the business. Such assets include the following accounts :

• Fixed or long term Assets

• Investments Assets

• Current Assets Account

✓ **Nominal Accounts :-** Certain expenses have to be incurred for carrying on the business. There are various incomes also in the business. Such accounts are known as nominal accounts.

❖ **Accounts of expenses include the following :**

E.g. Wages Account, Salary Account, Depreciation Account etc.

❖ **Accounts of incomes include :**

E.g. Interest received account, Discount received account, Dividend received account etc.

> ## Classification of Main (Important) Accounts:

PERSONAL A/C	REAL A/C	NOMINAL A/C
H.L.College of Commerce	Cash A/c	Carriage Inward A/c
Shah Medical Stores A/c	Machinery A/c	Carriage Outward A/c
Debtor's A/c	Furniture A/c	Wages A/c
Creditor's A/c	Building A/c	Interest Received A/c
Dayaben Gada's A/c	Patent A/c	Rent Paid A/c
Government of India A/c	Share Investment A/c	Discount Received A/c
Capital A/c	Goodwill A/c	Bad debts A/c
Drawings A/c	Copyright A/c	Loss due to goods destroy by fire A/c
Kalol Branch's A/c	Dead Stock A/c	Commission Received A/c
Dena Bank's A/c	Stationary Stock A/c	Commission Given A/c
IFFCO A/c	Gold & Silver A/c	Discount Allowed A/c

General India Insurance Co.Ltd A/c	Debenture A/c	Charity A/c
Gujarat University A/c	Bill Receivable A/c	Salary A/c
Bank Loan A/c	Bill Payable A/c	Stationary A/c
Sports Club's A/c	Closing Goods Stock a/c	Royalty A/c
A.G.High School's A/c	Petty Cash A/c	Expense of goods distributed as free samples A/c
Yogeshbhai Patel's A/c	Postal Savings Certificate A/c	Demurrage A/c
Unpaid Salary A/c	Kisan Vikas Patra A/c	Darmayo A/c
Prepaid Rent A/c	Shares of Reliance A/c	Bank Charges A/c
Life Insurance Premium A/c	Bank Fixed Deposit A/c	Bank Interest A/c
Income Tax A/c	Goodwill A/c	Railway Freight A/c
Bank Overdraft A/c	Telephone Deposit	Octroi A/c

	A/c	
Status Education's A/c	Trademark A/c	Depreciation A/c
		Machinery Repairs A/c
		Bad debts recovered A/c
		Dividend received A/c
		Debenture interest A/c
		Sales tax A/c
		Interest on Drawings A/c
		Interest on Capital A/c
		interest on borrowed Loan a/c
		Insurance Premium A/c
		General Reserve A/c

❖ **Rules of Debit and Credit :**

The word Double Entry System of accounting shows two effects or dual effect as seen earlier, every accounting transaction has two effects and it affects at least two accounts.

✓ **Rule for Personal Accounts : "Debit the receiver, Credit the giver ."**

If a personal account is associated with an accounting transaction, then determine whether that person is the receiver of the benefit (consideration) or the giver of the benefit.

E.g. Sold goods of **Rs. 5,000** to Anjana.

⇒ Anjana is receiver → According to rule of personal account "Debit the receiver" → Anjana's account debited.

✓ **Rule for Real Accounts : "Debit what comes in, Credit what goes out."**

If a goods or an asset account is associated with an accounting transaction then if a goods or asset come into the business, it (goods or asset) is debited. If goods assets go out of the business, it is credited.

E.g. Purchased furniture of **Rs. 1,000** for cash.

(1) Furniture comes in → According to rule of real account "Debit what comes in,

Credit what goes out."→ Furniture account debited

(2) Cash goes out → Cash account credited

✓ **Rule for Nominal Accounts : " Debit the expenses and losses, Credit the incomes and gains."**

When due to an accounting transaction. Business receives a gain or an income, then that account is credited, if business suffers a loss or incurs an expense, then that account is debited.

E.g. Paid salary of **Rs. 1,500**.

⇒ Salary is an expenses → According to rule debit the expenses → salary account debited.

⇒ **Steps of determine of debit or credit an account :**

1) **Determine the given transaction is economic or non-economic.:**

If the given transaction is non-economic then it is not recorded in the books of accounts, but the given transaction is economic then it is recorded and go to further step-**2**.

2) **Determine which two accounts are affected :**

If the given transaction is cash transaction then always one a/c is cash or bank a/c affected, but the given transaction is credit transaction then always one a/c is debtor's or creditor's a/c affected.

3) **Determine the types of accounts :**

♣ Personal A/C : accounts of individuals, sole proprietorship, partnership, banks, companies, schools, trusts, co-operative societies.

♣ Real A/C : Accounts relating to goods and assets.

♣ Nominal A/C : Accounts relating to expenses or losses and incomes or gain.

4) **Apply the rules of debit and credit, then record the transaction:**

• **Personal A/c :**

"Debit the receiver, Credit the giver."

- **Real A/c :**

  " Debit what comes in, Credit what goes out."

- **Nominal A/c :**

  "Debit the expenses and losses, Credit the incomes and gains ."

☐ PRACTICAL SECTION ☐

1. In the books of Dharti for the following transactions which account will you debit and which account will you credit ? Also give the resons :

   1. Took goods of **Rs. 200** for personal use.

   2. Purchased furniture of **Rs. 5000** from indraprashtha furniture mart.

   3. Paid **Rs. 1500** to Chandra for salary.

   4. Bank sent an advice for bank charges **Rs. 30.**

2. **Classify the following accounts :**

   1. Railway freight account

   2. Stationary Stock account

   3. Deprecation account

   4. Dividend received account

   5. Prepaid rent account

   6. Debenture account

   7. Bank overdraft

   8. Telephone deposit account

   9. General Reserve account

3.   **In the books of Galaxy for the following transaction, which account will you debit and credit ? Also give the reasons :**

✓   Paid **Rs. 1,000** to Motu for salary.

✓   Sold goods of **Rs. 10,500** to Mahesh on credit.

✓   Opened accurred account in SBI by depositing **Rs. 5,000**.

✓   Paid **Rs. 700** for brokerage.

✓   Seema returned goods of **Rs. 900**.

✓   Purchased goods of **Rs. 4,500** from Munni.

............xxxxxxxxx.........

CHAPTER - 4

" JOURNAL~JOURNALISING "

☐ THEORY SECTION ☐

❖ **Meaning of Journal :**

The journal is the basic book in double entry book-keeping system. It is the fundamental book on the basis of which all other books of accounts are written.

The English word ' **journal**' has its origin in Latin, where it means **'record'** or **'diary'**. Hence, the journal is the basic book or the book of original entry.

French word **'jour'** means **'day'**. Hence **'journal'** means a record of the daily transactions of the business.

⇒ **Specimen of Journal :**

Journal of Shri.........

Date	Particulars	Ledger Folio No. (L.F.)	Debit Rs.	Credit Rs.

❖ **Characteristics of Journal :**

✓ Journal is the first and basic book of accounts.

✓ According to the rules of debit and credit, the dual effect of an accounting transaction is recorded in it.

✓ Two columns are kept for writing the amount. The amount of the account to be debited is written in the debit amount column and the amount of the account to be credited is written in the credit amount column.

✓ The transactions are recorded daily in the journal and chronologically in the order of the date.

✓ Immediately, below a journal entry written in the journal, a brief explanation of the transaction is given in the brackets as narration so that the detailed information about the journal entry is also available.

❖ **Importance (Advantages) of Journal :**

➢ As the transactions are recorded in the journal in the order of time and date , no transactions is left out from recording.

➢ A record of all the transactions is kept systematically in the journal, so useful details are available when required.

➢ Since a brief explanation (narration) of every transaction is written, the details of every transaction can be referred to even after a long period.

➢ Two separate columns are kept in the journal for debit and credit amounts. Hence while posting there is no difficulty about which account should be debited and which account should be credited.

➢ **Important points :**

1) **Combined Entry:** "Generally, for every economic transaction separate entry is to be pass, but sometimes during a day one account is debited or credited more than once in a number of transactions, then it will be

convenient to pass only one entry for these transactions. This kind of entry is known as combined entry."

In short, " In any economic transaction at a time when two or more accounts are involved, a combined entry is passed."

2) **Transactions relating to Capital and Drawing:**

✓ If the owner of the business brings cash ,goods, debtors and assets in capital while starting the business always capital account is credited.

(Capital Account amount = Total Assets – Total Liabilities.)

✓ If the owner of the business has taken away any amount of cash, goods, assets for personal use always drawing account debited.

3) **Transactions relating to goods account :**

No.	Transaction	Effect
1.	When goods are purchased	Purchased A/c
2.	When we return goods from the goods purchased	Purchased Returns A/c
3.	When goods are sold	Sales A/c
4.	When customer returns goods from goods sold to him	Sales Returns A/c
5.	When the owner of the business takes goods for personal use	Goods gone as drawing A/c

6.	When goods are given in charity	Goods given in charity A/c
7.	When goods are distributed as samples for advertisement	Goods distributed as sample A/c
8.	When goods received as free samples in the business are sold	Sales A/c
9.	When goods are destroyed in fire	Goods destroyed by fire A/c
10.	When goods are stolen away	Goods stolen away A/c
11.	When goods destroyed due to rain	Goods destroyed due to rain A/c
12.	When goods destroyed due to an accident	Goods destroyed in accident A/c

♣ **When goods burnt by fire and such goods are not insured then :**

Loss due to fire A/c   Dr
  To Goods destroyed by fire A/c

♣ **If such goods are fully insured and insurance company accept full amount then:**

Loss due to fire A/c   Dr

Insurance Co. A/c   Dr

    To Goods destroyed by fire A/c

♣ **If such goods are fully insured but insurance company does not accept full amount then:**

    Insurance Co. A/c   Dr

        To Goods destroyed by fire A/c

4) **Transaction relating to Bad debts and Bad debts Recovered :**

➢ Journal entry for Bad debts :

    Bad debts A/c   Dr

        To Debtor's A/c

➢ Journal entry for Bad debts Recovered :

    Cash/Bank A/c   Dr

        To Bad debts Recovered   A/c

5) **Trade discount, Cash discount and Allowance:**

♣ **Trade discount :** "The manufacturing units decides the retail price of their products, so that in the open market it is available at the same rate. This retail price is known as maximum retail price. This price is known as catalogue price. To allow sufficient margin to the retailers ,companies to sell their goods at some lower rate the catalogue price to retailers which is known as trade discount." **Trade discount amount is not recorded in the books of accounts.**

♣ **Cash discount :**   "In the competitive market it is necessary to sell the goods on credit. But credit transaction creates a problem of liquidity in the business. To solve this problem, to provide incentive for immediate payment of goods sold, according to the tradition and custom of the business, some discount is given which is known as cash discount."

Cash discount amount is recorded in the books of accounts.

♣ **Difference between Trade discount and Cash discount.**

No.	Points	Trade Discount	Cash Discount
1.	Reason	Trade discount is allowed by a wholesaler to retailer, so that retailer is able to get sufficient profit.	Cash discount is allowed by the receiver of cash to the payer for the payment within credit period or for early payment.
2.	Calculation	Trade discount is calculated on the printed or the catalogue price.	Trade discount is calculated on the Net price of the bill.(Net price = Printed price – Trade discount.)
3.	Record in	Trade discount is not recorded in the books	Cash discount is recorded in the

	the books	of accounts.	books of accounts.
4.	Purpose	The purpose of trade discount is to retailer to sell goods at printed price.	The purpose of cash discount is prompt payment or for payment of cash within the credit period allowed.
5.	Deduction while preparing the bill	Trade discount is deducted while preparing the bill or invoice on purchase or sale of goods.	Cash discount is not deducted while preparing the bill or invoice.

♣ **Allowance :** "Sometimes trader allows some special reduction at the time of settlement of an account which is known as allowance." **Allowance amount is recorded in the books of accounts.**

☐ PRACTICAL SECTION ☐

1. **Pass the journal entries of Shri Dinaben Patel form the following transactions :**

    2011, June 1 Started business by bringing in cash **Rs. 1,60,000** debtors of **Rs. 40,000** , machinery of Rs. **1,00,000**, creditors of **Rs. 35,000** and stock of goods of **Rs. 20,000.**

1. Expense of **Rs. 3,000** was incurred at the time of inauguration.

2. Borrowed a loan of **Rs. 90,000** from Tulsi at **10 %** interest.

3. Deposited **Rs. 80,000** with the bank and opened an account.

4. Purchased furniture of **Rs. 20,000** from Sujal Furniture Mart.

5. Purchased tables, chairs and fan from Royal & Co. for **Rs. 5000** and paid through cheque.

6. Purchased goods of **Rs. 60,000** from Ketrina Distributors on credit at **10 %** trade discount.

7. Sold goods costing **Rs. 30,000** purchased from Ketrina Distributors after adding **20 %** profit to karina at **10 %** trade Discount.

8. Purchased goods of **Rs. 1,00,000** from Ram at **10 %** trade discount and **10 %** cash discount. Gave a cheque for half the amount.

9. Karina returned goods of **Rs. 1,080** of the goods sold her, which were returned to Ketrina Distributors.

10. Sold goods of **Rs. 40,000** purchased from Ram after adding **25 %** profit to Gunjan at **10 %** tarde discount and **10 %** cash discount. Received half the amount in cash.

11. Sold goods to Sujata for **Rs. 30,000** on credit and paid cartage **Rs. 400** in cash on her behalf.

12. Sold goods of **Rs. 40,000** after adding **30 %** profit to Palav at **10 %** trade discount and **10 %** cash discount, if the payment is made within **10** days.

13. Paid wages **Rs. 600** for whitewashing the shop.

14. Paid fire insurance premium **Rs. 500** and life insurance premium **Rs. 600** by cheque.

15.   Gave cash **Rs.100** and goods of **Rs. 300** to an orphanage.

15. Gunjan returned goods of **Rs. 1,350.**

16.   On the occasion of the celebration of the Independence Day, paid cash **Rs. 300** for refreshment expenses at the Traders Association.

17.   Goods returned by Gunjan were returned to Ram.

18.   Withdrew cash **Rs. 3,000** from the bank for office expenses.

19.   Received goods of **Rs. 600** as free samples.

20.   Goods received as free samples were given free to customers for advertisement.

21.   Received a cheque for half the amount from Palav. Allowed discount to him.

22.   Purchased a machine of **Rs. 10,000** and paid **Rs. 300** as wages for installing the machine.

23.   Distributed goods of **Rs. 400** as free samples.

24.   Received **Rs. 600** for brokerage and commission Received Personal dividend **Rs. 1,400** which was deposited in the business bank account.

25.   Issued a cheque to Ketrina Distributors after deducting an allowance of **Rs. 200**, to settle the account.

26.   Gunjan settled the account after deducting and allowance of **Rs. 150.**

27.   Palav gave cash **Rs. 10,000** and a cheque for the remaining amount to settle the account.

28.   Goods of **Rs. 6,000** were destroyed by fire, for which the insurance company accepted a claim for **Rs. 4,000.** Received **Rs. 400** on sale of goods destroyed by fire.

29. Goods of **Rs. 1,200** got wet in rain, on sale of which received **Rs. 400.** Goods of **Rs. 600** were stolen away.

30. Paid salary **Rs. 4,000** to the accountant and wages **Rs. 1,000** to per month to the worker. Paid telephone bill **Rs. 400** and light bill **Rs. 600** in cash. Paid interest on Tulsi's loan for two month. Sold goods of cost price **Rs. 12,000** for cash so as to earn **20 %** profit on sales price.

2) **From the following information prepare journal of Kumar and draw necessary accounts in ledger and find out its balance and state how much and which it is.**

1 Brought business **Rs. 18,000** cash **Rs. 7,000** receivables and a loan from rajendra shroff **Rs. 15,000.**

2 Opened bank account with Dena bank by depositing **Rs. 13,700.**

3 Cash sales **Rs. 4,900** and cash purchases

4 Paid **Rs. 3,200** for food exp in Vrudhashram (house for old aged oersons) on occasion of death anniversary of Grandfather.

5 Offered **Rs. 500** in temple on occasion of Patosava (Religious Festival).

6 Against the received of **Rs. 2,010** from Mansukhbhai, a cheque of **Rs. 2,000** is received which is deposited in the bank.

7 Paid **Rs. 1,100** cash and a cheque of **Rs. 1,000** to Jinalben against payables.

8 Bank has collected and credited **Rs. 1,200** in passbook, for the dividend of Samrat Ltd shares.

9 Paid sales tax of **Rs. 1,500** and income tax of **Rs. 4,000** by cheque.

10 Withdrew **Rs. 1,000** from bank to pay to Mamta.

11 Against the dues of **Rs. 1,030** paid **Rs. 1,000** to Chandrikaben.

12 On occasion of a birthday of Neha, paid **Rs. 700** to ram bakery for cake.

13 A cheque of **Rs. 1,600** of Ila agency is collected by bank and credited in pass book. For this a bank commission of **Rs. 20** is debit in pass book by bank.

3) **Pass journal entries for the business transactions of " shah Stores " started by Shri Arya shah.**

2004.

June-1 Started business by bringing in cash**Rs. 30000** stock of goods of **Rs. 10000** debtors of **Rs. 15000** and creditors of **Rs. 5000.**

June-4 Purchased furniture of **Rs. 12000** from " Jayshree mart " on credit paid cartage **Rs. 80** in cash.

June-7 Purchased balances and weights of **Rs. 1000.**

June-16 Goods of **Rs. 2000** were destroyed

June-21 Withdraw **Rs. 500** for household expenses and **Rs. 1500** for office expenses from bank.

June-24 Nirma Co. gave goods of **Rs. 300** as free samples, which were sold off for **Rs. 350.**

4) **Pass journal entries for the following transactions :**

- Brought Goods of **Rs. 3,000** and machine of **Rs. 5,000** to start the business.

- Purchased an old bicycle for **Rs. 600** from Mohan on one month credit.
- Rent of the shop **Rs. 1,000** in unpaid.
- Interest **Rs. 800** is due but not received.
- A payment of **Rs. 600** for interest is debited to purchase account
- Bad debts recovered **Rs. 800** were wrongly credited to the account of Reshma, who paid the amount.

5) **Write journal of the following transactions.**

1. Sold goods cost of **Rs. 8000** for cash so as to earn **20%** profit on sales price.
2. Paid cash **Rs. 300** as office rent and **Rs. 200** as house rent.
3. Paid life insurance premium **Rs. 350** and fire insurance premium **Rs. 450** by cheque.
4. Sold goods of **Rs. 12000** to Jay at **10%** trade discount and **10 %** cash discount received a cheque for half of the amount.

6) **Prepare the journal of Shri Mahavir from the following transactions.**

2011,March 1 Started business by bringing in cash **Rs. 75,000**, debtors of **Rs. 1,50,000**, building , **Rs. 5,00,000**, Stock of goods of **Rs. 15,000** and creditors of **Rs. 70,000**.

March **5** Deposited **Rs. 40,000** with the ICICI bank and Opened an account.

9 Purchased furniture of **Rs. 5,000** from Sunil Furniture Mart.

12 Purchased goods of **Rs. 9,000** from Nalin and paid half amount by Cheque.

15 Received goods of **Rs. 150** as free samples.

18 The bank credited interest **Rs. 200.**

20 Paid son's fees **Rs. 1,500** from the business.

22 Received commission **Rs. 500** .

23 Paid shop rent **Rs. 300** and residential rent **Rs. 700.**

27 Received **Rs. 800** dividend on shares of **" Hero Honda".**

28 Sold goods of **Rs. 16,000** to Ashish at **10 %** trade discount and **10 %** cash discount Received a cheque for half the amount.

29 withdrew **Rs. 2,500** for house hold expenses and **Rs. 3,500** for office expenses from bank.

30 Ashish returned goods of **Rs. 1,300** and paid the remaining amount in cash.

............xxxxxxxxx.........

CHAPTER - 5

"SUBSIDIARY BOOKS"

□ THEORY SECTION □

♣ **Definition :-** "subsidiary books mean sub-divided journals to record a group of respective transaction". A separate book for each such sub-division maintained.

♣ **Types of Subsidiary Books:-**
➢ Purchase book
➢ Sales book
➢ Purchase Returns book
➢ Cash book
➢ Petty Cash book
➢ Bills Receivable book
➢ Bills Payable book
➢ Journal proper

♣ **Advantages of Maintaining Subsidiary books:-**
✓ The size of journal can be reduced and it also facilitates easy recording of various transactions.
✓ The work of posting of transaction to individual accounts from subsidiary books becomes easier.

   At fixed interval, total of each subsidiary book can be posted directly into respective ledger account.

For example total of purchase book at the end of fixed interval (say, every month) can be posted as credit purchase on debit side of purchase account in the ledger.

✓ Due to benefit of division of work, accounts can be written by more than one person.

✓ Different persons can be entrusted responsibility of recording transactions in a particular subsidiary book.

✓ It is possible to record various transaction simultaneously by more than one person.

✓ Useful information is made available easily in lesser time.

✓ All transactions of same nature are recorded at one place and hence analysis therefore becomes easier.

This becomes very helpful to decision makers

✓ With the help of subsidiary books, auditing becomes easier and speedy.

✓ Subsidiary Books can also make work simple even where accounts are computerized.

♣ **Purchase Book :-**

We know that purchases can be mainly :

(1) Cash purchase (2) credit purchase.

• In purchase book, only transactions relating to credit purchase of respective goods are recorded . Transactions of cash purchase and purchases of assets are not recorded in purchase book.

Net amount of credit purchase of goods is recorded in purchase book.

Net Amount = Total amount of credit purchase of goods less trade discount.

When part payment is made in a credit purchase transaction, it will be easier to record the entire transaction as that of credit purchase.

Purchased book can be maintained in following two ways :

(1) Simple Purchase Book:-

When a business man is Purchasing only one type of goods, generally a simple purchase book is maintained.

Specimen of simple Purchase Book

Purchase Book of Shri………

Date	Name of supplier/ Particulars	Inward Invoice Number	L.F.	Amount Rs.
	Total Credit Purchase			

(2) Columnar Purchase Book :-

We have seen that columnar purchase book can be prepared in two ways. (1) According to types of goods and (2) Purchase book with columns for goods and expenses Let us study each of them.

(1) Purchase Book with columns according to types of goods :-

When he purchases goods of more than one type, columnar purchase book for each types of goods is prepared to know the detail and information about each variety of goods .

Purchase Book of Shri.........

Date	Name of supplier/ Particulars	Inward Invoice Number	L.F	Amount Rs.			Total Rs.
				Table	Chair	Sofas	
Total Credit Purchase							

(2) **Purchase book with columns for goods and expenses :** When a businessman purchase goods on credit, many times , the seller prepares his invoice by adding various other charges apart from the value of goods. Normally, such charges are in respect of sales tax, mahajan lago, railway freight, octroi, carriage , etc.

Date	Name of supplier	Inward Invoice Number	L. F.	Amount Rs.				Total Rs.
				Goods Net Rs.	Sales Tax Rs.	Mahajan Lago Rs.	Octroi Rs.	
Total Credit Purchase								

♣ **Sales Book :-**

Goods are generally sold in two ways.

(1) Credit sales and (2) Cash sales.

Only transactions of credit sales of goods by the enterprise are recorded in sales book. Transactions of cash sales or sale of assets are not recorded in sales book.

(1) Simple Sales Book :-

When a businessman is selling only one type of goods, generally a simple sales book is maintained.

Specimen of simple Sales Book

Sales Book of Shri.........

Date	Name of Customer /Particulars	Outward Invoice	L.F. Number	Amount Rs.

		Number		
	Total Credit Purchase			

(2)   Columnar Sales Book :-

We have seen that columnar purchase book can be prepared in two ways. (1) According to types of goods and (2) Purchase book with columns for goods and expenses Let us study each of them.

(1)   Sales Book with columns according to types of goods

Sales Book of Shri.........

Date	Name of supplier/ Particulars	Outward Invoice Number	L.F	Amount Rs.			Total
				Table	Chair	Sofas	
Total Credit Purchase							

When he purchases goods of more than one type, columnar purchase book for each types of goods is prepared to know the detail and information about each variety of goods .

(2) Sales book with columns for goods and expenses :

When a businessman purchase goods on credit, many times , the seller prepares his invoice by adding various other charges apart from the value of goods. Normally, such charges are in respect of sales tax, mahajan lago, railway freight, octroi, carriage , etc.

Sales Book of Shri.........

Date	Name of customer	Outward Invoice Number	L. F.	Amount Rs.				Total Rs.
				Goods Net Rs.	Sales Tax Rs.	Mahajan Lago Rs.	Octroi Rs.	
Total Credit Purchase								

♣ **Returns Book:-**

Returns book are of two types. (1) Purchase Return book (2) Sales Return Book.

(1) Purchase Return book :-

An enterprise purchase goods for its business. Sometimes, such goods have to be returned to the supplier for some reasons. Generally goods once purchased are returned under the following circumstances.

✓   When the goods are not as per sample.

✓   When goods are of inferior quality.

✓   When goods are in damaged condition.

✓   To get rebate or refund by returning container or packing of the goods.

✓   Goods returned for any other reason.

When goods purchased on credit are returned for any of the above stated reasons, such returns are recorded in purchase return book.

⇒ **Debit Note :** When goods purchased on credit are returned to the supplier, a letter with the reason and amount of goods returned is also sent along with goods returned by the customer. This letter is known as Debit Note.

Debit note is written in the following circumstances :

•   When goods purchased are in damaged condition, goods are not according to samples, goods are not inferior quality.

•   When the bill received from trader is more amount than the amount of actual goods purchased.

•   When goods sent by trader is more than the order placed.

Debit note is an important document for preparation of Purchased return book.

❖   Purchase return book can be mainly prepared in two ways :

(1) Simple purchase return book (2) Columnar purchase return book.

1) **Simple Purchase Return Book (For only types of goods)**

Purchase Return Book of Shri……..

Date	Name of supplier /Particulars	Debit Note No.	L.F. Number	Amount Rs.
Total Credit Purchase Returns				

2) **Columnar Purchase Book :-**

We have seen that columnar purchase return book can be prepared in two ways. (1) According to types of goods and (2) Purchase return book with columns for goods and expenses

Let us study each of them.

1) According to types of goods

Purchase Return Book of Shri……..

Date	Name of supplier/ Particulars	Outward Invoice Number	L.F	Amount Rs.			Total Rs.
				Table	Chair	Sofas	

Total Credit Purchase				

2) Purchase return book with columns for goods and expenses.

Purchase Return Book of Shri...

Date	Name of supplier	Debit Note Number	L. F.	Amount Rs.				Total Rs.
				Goods Net Rs.	Sales Tax Rs.	Mahajan Lago Rs.	Octroi Rs.	
	Total Credit Purchase							

(2) **Sales Return Book:** An enterprise records transaction of goods returned in sales return book if the goods sold on credit are returned by its customers. Generally goods once sold are returned under the following circumstances.

✓ When the goods are not as per sample.

✓ When goods are of inferior quality.

✓ When goods are in damaged condition.

✓ To get rebate or refund by returning container or packing of the goods.

✓ Goods returned for any other reason.

When goods sold on credit are returned for any of the above stated reasons, such returns are recorded in sales return book.

❖ Sales return book can be mainly prepared in two ways :

(1) Simple sales return book (2) Columnar sales return book.

1. Simple Sales Returns Book (For only types of goods)

Sales Return Book of Shri........

Date	Name of Customer /Particulars	Credit Note No.	L.F. Number	Amount Rs.
Total Credit Sales Returns				

(2) Columnar Sales Book :-

We have seen that columnar purchase return book can be prepared in two ways. (1) According to types of goods and (2) Sales book with columns for goods and expenses Let us study each of them.

(1) According to types of goods

Date	Name of Customer /Particulars	Credit Note No.	L.F.	Amount Rs.			Total Rs.
				Table	Chair	Sofas	

				Amount Rs.				Total Rs.
	Total Credit Sales Returns							

Sales book with columns for goods and expenses

Date	Name of Customer	Credit Note Number	L. F.	Amount Rs.				Total Rs.
				Goods Net Rs.	Sales Tax Rs.	Mahajan Lago Rs.	Octroi Rs.	
	Total Credit Purchase							

⇒ **Credit Note:** When goods sent on credit are returned by the customer, a letter is sent to him by the trader with the reasons for crediting customer's account is known as Credit Note.

Credit note is written in the following circumstances :

- When goods sent are in damaged condition, goods are not according to samples, goods are not inferior quality.

- When some mistakes has taken place in calculation and the bill sent to him with some more amount than the actual one.
- When goods sent by trader is more than the order placed.

Credit note is an important document for preparation of Sales return book.

♣ Difference between Debit Note and Credit Note:

No.	Debit Note	Credit Note
1.	When goods purchased are returned, purchaser sent a letter containing information related to the returns transaction, it is known as debit note.	When goods sold are returned by customer and trader sent a letter stating details of returns transaction, it is known as credit note.
2.	The writer of the debit note, debited the account of trader and credited the account purchase return.	The writer of the credit note, credited the account of customer and debited the account sales return.
3.	When there is a change in the amount of a bill, because of some reason, then purchaser sent the	When there is a change in the amount of a bill, noted by the customer, the seller sent credit note

	debit note with the difference of amount to seller.	to the customer with the difference of amount to seller.
4.	A debit note is written for person from whom some rebate is to be claimed.	A credit note is writte for person to whom some rebate is to be given.

☐ PRACTICAL SECTION ☐

1) From the following information prepare Subsidiary books of Binal and post them in necessary accounts:

1. Goods of **Rs. 4,500** are sold at **25%** profit to shakila through outward invoice number **321**.

2. goods of **Rs. 4,800** are purchased from Nafisa at **10%** trade discount-inward invoice number **133**.

3. Goods of **Rs.2,800** are sold at **15 %** profit to Nasim. Outward invoice number **322**.

4. Goods of **Rs.3,000** are purchased from Pravin, at **5 %** trade discount. Inward invoice number **255**.

5. Three cupboards at the rate of **Rs. 2,300** are purchased from Ayesha furniture mart. Credit memo (bill) no **125**.

6. As one of the cupboards from those which were purchased from Ayesha furniture mart, is in damaged condition, is returned to them. Debit note number **105**.

7. Goods of **Rs.300** are returned to Vasanben with a debit note no **106**.

8. Goods of **Rs. 250** are received back from Bhakti credit note no **181**.

9. As the goods of **Rs. 380** are damaged are returned it Nafisa debit note no **107**.

10. As the goods of **Rs. 550** were not according to sample Nasim has returned the goods. Credit note no **182**.

2) From the following transactions prepare purchase book sales book, purchase returns book and sales return book in the books of Shri Amrutlal.

2003.

June-1 Purchased good of **Rs.8000** from ramesh at **10 %** trade discount under bill number **17**.

June-2 Purchased goods of **Rs. 5000** from Naresh at **10 %** cash discount on one month's credit.

June- 5 Sold goods of **Rs. 10000** to Pnkaj at **5 %** trade discount and **2 %** cash discount Bill no. **13**

June-7 Purchased goods of **Rs.7000** from market cash memo no.**15**.

June-9 Sold goods of **Rs.7000** to Nina at **10 %** trade discount on two month's credit. Sent bill number **24** after adding carriage charges of **Rs.100**.

June10 Sold goods of **Rs. 11000** in market cash memo no **180**

June 11 Pankaj returned goods of **Rs.2000** for which credit note number **10** was sent to him.

June 13 Retuned goods of **Rs.1500** to ramesh along with debit not no **8**.

June 15 Purchased furniture of **Rs.11000** kalpana furniture mart.

June 16 Purchased goods of **Rs.12000** from Chandravadan and paid half of the amount immediately.

June 17 Sold to Alpa for **Rs. 14000** the entire goods purchased from Chandarvadan credit **3** months and trade discount **10 %**.

June 19 Alpa returned half of the goods sold to her and the same were returned to Chandravadan

June 22 Kanak placed an order for supply of goods of **Rs.6000** at **10 %** trade discount

June 24 Supplied goods to Kanak as per his order under invoice number **71**.

June 28 Cash purchase **Rs.14000** cash sales **Rs.20000**.

June 30 Nina returned half of the goods sold to her and it was agreed to give rebate of **Rs.50** towards carriage.

3)   **2009, April 1** Purchased from Priya Corporation goods of **Rs.10,000** at **10 %** trade discount. Sales tax at **5%**, Railway freight **Rs.150**, Mahajan Lago **Rs.30**. Invoice no.**11**.

   3. Purchased goods of **Rs.8,000** From Paresh traders, sales tax at **5%**, railway freight **Rs.100** andcarriage **Rs.50**.

   5.   Sold goods of **Rs.6,000** to mala corporation at **10 %** trade discount. Sales tax at **10 %**, Carriage **Rs.30** railway freight **Rs.30**. Bill no.**713**.

   8. Sold entire goods purchased from Paresh traderds to Mita traders at **25 %** profit on cost, on two month's credit. charged sales tax at **5%**, mahajan lago **Rs.20**,railway freight **Rs. 150**,carriage **Rs.50**.

11. Mala corporation returned **50 %** of goods and they were given credit for sales tax **Rs.270**, railway freight **Rs. 50** and carriage **Rs.10**. Credit no. **11**

15. Sold goods of **Rs.10,000** Chandra traders at **10 %** trade discount. Sales tax **2%**, carriage **Rs.50** and railway freight **Rs.100**. Bill no **100**.

21. Purchased Furniture of **Rs.5,000** from Vinod. Received bill with **10 %** sales tax.

25. Mita traders returned half of the goods. Gave credit of sales tax **Rs.250**, Railway freight **Rs.50** and carriage **Rs.20**. Credit note no **12**.

28. Goods returned by Mita traders were returned to Paresh trader debit note no **10**.Rebate for sales tax of **Rs. 200**, railway freight of **Rs.50** and carriage of **Rs.20** will be received in is to be allowed by Paresh.

4) **Prepare purchase Book, Sales book, purchase Returns book and sales return book in the books of Kumar sports from the following transactions :**

2003

June 1 Sold goods of **Rs.10,000** to Kapil at **10 %** trade discount on one month's credit under bill No.**130**.

June 3. Purchased from Sunil goods of **Rs. 20,000** at **10 %** trade discount on one month's credit under bill No**11**.

June 4. Out of goods purchased from Sunil sold half of the goods (Before deducting discount) to Gavasakar adding **25 %** profit on cost. Credit allowed **2 Months**.

June 8. Sold goods of **Rs.8,000** to Rohan for cash at **2%** cash discount.

June 11. Purchased goods of **Rs.40,000** from Vinod on two month's credit. Vinod sent bill no. **1147** charging sales tax at **5 %** and **50 %** of the amount was paid to him.

June 14. Gavaskar returned half of the goods sold to him. This was returned to Sunil by us. Send credit note no. **14** to Gavaskar and debit note no. **5** to Sunil.

June 18. Purchased a machine from Azhar for **Rs.14,000** on two months credit.

June 21. Sold to Sangeeta goods of **Rs.7,000** at **10 %** trade discount under bill no. **134** on one month'scredit.

June 23. Sangeeta returned entire goods and we sent a credit note no. **15** to her. Sent other goods of **Rs.3,000** to Sangeeta for which she made payment immediately by cheque.

June 25. Placed an order with Juhi for supply of goods of **Rs. 8,000** at **5%** trade discount.

June 26. Bhaskar placed an order for supply of goods of **Rs. 10,000** at **5 %** trade discount.

June 30. All the goods for which order was placed with Juhi were sent by Juhi directly to Bhaskar as per our instruction to supply goods to Bhaskar as per his order.

............×××××××××.........

CHAPTER -6

"CASH BOOK"

THEORY SECTION

⇒ **Meaning:**

Cash book is prepared to record cash transaction and also to know the cash balance at the end of a day or at the end of specific time period.

⇒ According to the necessity of any business or profession, cash book can be prepared as per any one of the following three types :

❖ **Simple Cash Book:** In simple cash book, only transaction involving receipts and payments of cash are recorded. Specimen of simple cash book as under:

Cash Book of Shri………….

Date	Receipts	Receipt No.	L.F.	Amount	Date	Payments	Voucher No.	L.F.	Amount
	To Balance (B/f) **RECEIPTS**					**PAYAMENTS** By Balance (C/f)			

❖ **Two-columnar Cash Book**

➤ **Cash and discount columnar :**

Specimen of Cash and discount columnar as under:

Cash Book of Shri………….

Date	Receipts	R.	L. F.	Dis. Allowed	Cash	Date	Payments	V.	L. F.	Discount Received	Cash
	To Balance (B/f) Receipts						Payments By Balance (C/f)				

➤ **Cash and bank columnar:**

Specimen of Cash and bank columnar cash book as under:

Cash Book of Shri…………..

Date	Receipts	R.	L.F.	Cash	Bank	Date	Payments	V. No.	L.F.	Cash	Bank
	To Balance (B/f) **RECEIPTS**						Payments Balance (C/f)				

> ➢ **Bank and discount columnar:**

Specimen of Bank and discount columnar book as under:

Cash Book of Shri…………..

Date	Receipts	Receipt No.	L.F.	Amount	Date	Payments	Voucher No.	L.F.	Amount
	To Balance (B/f) **RECEIPTS**					**PAYAMENTS** By Balance (C/f)			

⇒ **Three-columnar cash book (Cash, discount and bank columnar cash book):**

In this type of cash book, three columns of amount are kept on both the sides discount column, cash column and bank column. in this type of cash book, cash and bank transactions and discount received and allowed are recorded in the same structure.

Specimen of three columnar Cash book as under:

Cash Book of Shri..............

Date	Receipts	R. N.	L. F.	D. A.	Cash	Bank	Date	Payments	V. N.	L. F.	D. R.	Cash	Bank
	Balance (B/f)							**Payments**					
	Receipts							Balance (C/f)					

⇒ **Advantages of Cash Book:-**

✓ As the structure of cash book is like a ledger account, it serves the purpose of both journal and ledger account. Therefore, time and labor are saved as cash account need not be prepared in the ledger when the cash book is maintained.

✓ Cash book is maintained separate from the journal, therefore, the responsibility of preparing it can be definitely allotted to a different person and the benefit of division of labor can be obtained.

✓ Cash balance can be known daily or at the end of the given period by maintaining the cash book.

✓ If the balance of cash book (account) is worked out daily, then the physical cash balance can be compared with it and any error or cash embezzlement can be known immediately.

✓ As per the requirement of business, the nature and volume of transactions cash book can be prepared in various different types. If three-columnar cash book is prepared, then the transactions of cash, bank and discount can be recorded and therefore, separate bank account also need not be prepared.

⇒ **Contra Transactions :**

In this type of transactions both, cash and bank account are involved. "Contra transaction" means such financial transaction, in which cash and bank, both the accounts get affected, this type of transaction is recorded on both the side of cash book.

⇒ **Contra transactions are of two types :-**

➤ **Cash deposited in the bank :**

When the cash is deposited in the bank, cash balance is on one hand and bank balance is increased on the other hand.

➤ **Cash withdrawn from the bank :-**

When the cash is withdrawn from the bank cash balance is increased on one hand and bank balance is reduced on the other hand.

⇒ **Petty Cash Book :-**

"The book kept by the petty cashier for keeping a record for payment of such expenses like postage, tea and refreshment expenses, stationary expenses etc. is known as **Petty Cash Book.**"

Petty cashier prepares the petty cash book, in which separate columns are maintained for various expenses to be paid by the petty cashier. So that the information of various expenses to be paid by the petty cashier is available.

Types of petty Cash book : Cash book can be prepared in two types:

1) Simple petty Cash book

2) Petty cash book on impress system.

❖ **Simple petty Cash book :-**

In this type of petty cash book, the petty cashier is given a fixed amount in the beginning. At the end of a given period the main cashier gives more cash if required. As and when the expenses are paid, they are recorded in the petty cash book.

Specimen of Simple Petty Cash book as under:

Petty Cash Book of Shri…………..

Rec Eipts	Date	Parti.	V. N	Total Rs.	Particulars of Various Expenses		L. F	Personal		
					Wages/ Stationary	Postage	Tea Ref.	Carriage	Mis. exp	
		Bal. (B/f)								

❖ **Petty cash book on impress system:-**

In this type of petty cash book affixed amount is given at the beginning of the fixed period by the main cashier to the petty cashier. Petty cashier makes the payment for various expenses from the amount so received and keeps the record of such expenses. At the end of the fixed period, the petty cashier gives the accounts of the expenses paid by him to the main cashier. The main cashier provides cash equal to the amount spent by the petty cashier at the beginning of the next period so that again the pre decided fixed balance remains with the petty cashier at the beginning of the next period in this type, as fixed amount of cash balance is maintained at the beginning of each period it is known as impress system of petty cash book.

☐ **PRACTICAL SECTION** ☐

1) From the following transactions, prepare two columner bank book having columns of State Bank of India (SBI) and Bank of Baroda (BOB) in that books of Munmun.

Jan. 1. Opening bank overdraft- SBI **Rs. 6,000** opening bank balance BOB **Rs. 4,000.**

4. Goods of **Rs. 4,000** sold, for which a cheque is received, which is deposited in the bank account of SBI.

5. Goods of **Rs. 6,000** are purchased, for which cheques of **Rs. 2,000** on BOB and **Rs. 4,000** on SBI are issued towards payment.

7. Salary of **Rs. 14,000** paid by cheque of SBI.

11. SBI credited **Rs. 500** for bank interest and **Rs. 2,500** after collecting dividend in the bank account.

13. Cheque of **Rs. 7,000** is received from Anuj towards payment of an old debt.

15. Cheque received from Anuj's is deposited in the bank account of BOB.

18. Cheque of **Rs. 3,000** issued from bank account of BOB, is deposited in the bank account of SBI.

23. Goods of **Rs. 2,500** purchased, for which cheque of the entire amount is issued from the BOB bank account.

26. Machine of **Rs. 6,000** purchased, **50 %** amount is paid by cheque of SBI and for the remaining amount, a cheque of BOB is issued.

2) **From the following transactions, prepare three columnar cash book of Meeta.**

August 1. Opening bank balance **Rs. 5,000** and opening cash balance **Rs. 1,000.**

3. Goods of **Rs. 10,000** sold to Nirma at **10 %** trade discount, for which the amount is received by cheque.

5. Cheque issued by Nirma is dishonoured.

7. Receiver of Nirma paid dividend of **50 paise** in a rupee by cash.

9. Goods of **Rs. 6,000** sold to Karishma by cash. Cash discount of 10 % is to be given.

13. Goods of **Rs. 5,000** purchased from Pravina at 10% cash discount. Half of the amount is paid by cash and remaining amount is paid by cheque.

15. Bank has collected a dividend of **Rs. 1,000** and credited in our account.

17. Bank has credited **Rs. 40** towards bank interested in our account.

24. Advertisement expenses of **Rs. 3,000** paid by cash.

26. **Rs. 1,000** withdrawn from the business for personal us

27. **Rs. 3,000** paid by cheque for goods purchased for personal use.

28. Viral has been given s cheque of **Rs. 3,000** in full settlement of account of **Rs. 3,045.**

29. Jigna has paid by cheque **Rs. 2,500** in full settlement of account of **Rs. 2,575.**

31. After keeping cash on hand of **Rs. 2,500** remaining amount is taken for personal use.

3) **From the following transactions prepare three columnar cash book of Mukti.**

2003.

May-1 Opening cash balances **Rs. 10000** opening bank overdraft **Rs. 3000.**

May-2 Goods of **Rs. 2000** purchased from Vipul at **10 %** cash discount and a cheque is issued for the necessary amount.

May-4 Goods of **Rs. 6000** purchased from Zarina at **10 %** trade discount half of the amount is paid by cash and the remaining amount is paid by cheque.

May-5 Salary of **Rs. 500** and stationery of **Rs. 800** are paid by cheque.

May-7 Rs. 4000 deposited in the bank.

May-8 Cheque of **Rs. 6000** is issued to Vidisha in full settlement of her account of **Rs. 6020.**

May-11 Paragi padi cash of **Rs. 6000** and a cheque of **Rs. 4000** in full settlement. of her account of **Rs. 10030.** The cheque is immedetialy deposited in the bank.

May-14 Cheque of **Rs. 3000** is received from Vasant towards payment of an old debt.

May-17 Deposited in the bank the cheque received from Vasant.

May-19 Cheque issued by Vasant is dishounoured.

May-21 A dividend at the rate of **50** paise per rupee is received from the receiver of Vasant.

May-23 Rs. 2000 paid towards income tax of Mukti.

May-29 Goods of **Rs. 10,000** sold to Mala at **10 %** cash discount. Mala issued a cheque for **60 %** of the amount and the remaining amount is paid by cash cheque received is immediately deposited in the bank.

May-31 After keeping cash on hand of **Rs. 1500** the balance amount is deposited in the bank.

4) **From the following information of Sewaram, prepare three columnar cash book and post it in ledger :**

2011

Dec 1. Cash balance **Rs. 11,000** and bank balance **Rs. 15,000.**

2. Withdrawn **Rs. 5,000** from bank for business

3. Cash purchases **Rs. 2,000** and cash sales **Rs. 6,000.**

4. Purchased files, ballpens etc. and gave a cheque of **Rs. 300.**

5. A cheque of **Rs. 1,500** is given to Yunus for full settlement towards payables of **Rs. 1,505.**

6. Against the receivables of **Rs. 2,320** due to from Sukhram received **Rs. 2,300** in full Settlement.

9. A cheque of **Rs. 900** is given to Divya Bhaskar newspaper for advertisement exp.

10. By paying cash of **Rs. 2,600** Panna has closed her account of **Rs. 2,630.**

11. Paid electricity bill of the shop **Rs. 1,600** and of the residence **Rs. 950.**

5) **From the following transactions prepare petty cash book for Rukmani.**

2003

Feb-1 Opening petty cash balance **Rs. 3000.**

Feb-1 Amount received from the chief cashier **Rs. 500.**

Feb-3 Wages of **Rs. 500** and carriage of are paid.

Feb-4 **Rs. 800** paid for postage and postal stamps expenses.

Feb-5 **Rs. 100** paid for wages.

Feb-7 Stationery Expenses paid **Rs. 200**

Feb-8 **Rs. 300** paid for tea and refreshment expenses.

Feb-9 **Rs. 900** received from the main cashier.

Feb-10 Misc. Exp paid **Rs. 100.**

Feb-11 **Rs. 200** given to Manoj for payment of misc. expenses.

6) **From the following transactions, prepare petty cash book of Harshil as per petty imprest system:-**

February

1. Cash received from the main cashier **Rs. 2,000**

2. **Rs. 400** for printing charges of bill book and **Rs. 100** for other stationery items are paid.

4 . Postage expenses paid **Rs. 100.**

5. Carriage of **Rs. 40** and Wages of **Rs. 50** Paid.

7. **Rs. 200**is advanced to Brij towards salary.

14. **Rs. 100** is given to Vishal for payment of misc expenses.

17. Carriage of **Rs. 10** and stationary expenses of **Rs. 200** are paid.

18. **Rs. 50** paid for misc expenses.

23. Postal stamps purchased for **Rs. 40.**

27. **Rs. 110** for Wages and **Rs. 50** for misc. expenses are paid.

7) Prepare Double Column Cash Book with cash and bank Columns from the following:

2003 Jan 1 Cash in hand **Rs. 22,000**

Cash at bank **Rs. 5,000.**

2 Sold goods for cash **Rs. 15,000.**

4 Cash withdrawn from bank **Rs. 2,000.**

5 Credit purchases from Deena **Rs. 15,000.**

6 Cash deposited into bank **Rs. 5,000.**

10 Paid wages by cheque **Rs. 10,000.**

14 Cash received from sale of furniture **Rs. 10,000** and out of it paid into bank **Rs. 2,000.**

18 Bank charges charged by the bank **Rs. 1,300.**

20 Cheque issued to Deena **Rs. 15,000.**

24 Received a cheque for **Rs. 1,000** from Pasubathy, Deposited into the bank.

28 Deena, to whom we have issued a cheque for credit purchases has reported that our cheque is dishonoured.

.............xxxxxxxxx.........

CHAPTER - 7

"JOURNAL PROPER"

☐ **THEORY SECTION** ☐

❖ **<u>Definition</u> :** "Generally, the transaction which are not recorded in the other subsidiary books, are recorded in one special subsidiary book known as **Journal Proper**."

⇒ The following types of transactions are included in the journal proper.

1. Opening journal entries.
2. Transaction which are not included in other subsidiary books.
3. Transaction of inter accounts transfer.
4. Closing entries.
5. Adjustment entries.
6. Rectification entries.

1) <u>Opening Journal Entries</u> :
"When a businessman starts his business, he brings his personal assets and liabilities in the business at that time it is necessary to make the entry which is known as opening entry." **Important Note : cash brought by the owner in while starting the business will not be recorded in Journal Proper because it will be recorded in the cash book.**

➤ Opening entry will be :

Assets A/c   Dr. (without cash)

      To Liabilities A/c

      To Capital   A/c

2) **Transaction Which are not Included in other Subsidiary Books :**

a) **Transaction of Credit Purchase or Credit Sale of an Assets :**

b) **Transactions for which Subsidiary Books are not kept**

✓ When bill accepted by the debtor of the business.

      Bills Receivable A/c   Dr.

         To Debtor   A/c

✓ When bill accepted by the owner from the creditors of the business.

      Creditor A/c   Dr.

         To Bills Payable   A/c

✓ When bill accepted by the debtor of the business is dishonoured.

      Debtor   A/c   Dr.

         To Bills Receivable A/c

c) **Special Transactions not Recorded in other Subsidiary Books :**

• Goods given in charity, as samples, goods taken for personal use.

• Dishonor of a bill and Bad debts

• Endorsement of bill receivable

• Loss of goods due to fire, accident, theft etc.

- Depreciation

3) **Transaction of Inter Accounts Transfer :** Sometimes because of some reasons when certain amount or total amount is to be transferred from one account to another account it is recorded in Journal Proper.

♣ For Depreciation on Machinery :

Depreciation A/c   Dr.

   To Machinery A/c

♣ For amount of drawing A/c is transferred to capital A/c

Capital A/c   Dr.

   To Drawing A/c

♣ For debtor agreed to pay amount to creditor of the business.

Creditor A/c   Dr.

   To Debtor A/c

4) **Closing Entries :** At the end of the year when journal entries are passed in journal proper to close the accounts, they are known as closing entries.

No.	Name of Account	Transferred To Which Account
1.	Purchase A/c (Cr)	Trading A/c (Dr)
2.	Purchase return A/c (Dr)	Trading A/c (Cr)
3.	Sales A/c (Dr)	Trading A/c (Cr)
4.	Sales return A/c (Cr)	Trading A/c (Dr)

5.	Wages, carriage inward, octroi (Exp. related to purchase) (Cr)	Trading A/c (Dr)
6.	Other expenses (Cr)	Profit and Loss A/c (Dr)
7.	Incomes (Dr)	Profit and Loss A/c (Cr)
8.	Opening stock (Cr)	Trading A/c (Dr)
9.	Closing stock (Dr)	Trading A/c (Cr)
10.	Gross Profit - Trading A/c (Dr)	Profit and Loss A/c (Cr)
11.	Gross Loss - Trading A/c (Cr)	Profit and Loss A/c (Dr)

5) Adjustment Entries : " At the end of the year certain accounting effects are yet to be given in order to know the true and fair financial position and the result of the business, at the time of preparing final accounts, these entries known as adjustment entries."

❖ For Closing Stock :
　　　Closing stock A/c　　Dr.
　　　　　To Trading A/c
❖ For Depreciation on Fixed Assets :
　　　Depreciation A/c　　Dr.
　　　　　To Fixed Assets A/c

❖ For Bad Debts :

      Bad debts A/c   Dr.

          To Debtor A/c

❖ For Outstanding/Unpaid Expenses : (E.g. Salary)

      Salary A/c   Dr.

          To Outstanding salary A/c

❖ For Prepaid Expenses : (E.g. Wages)

      Prepaid Wages A/c   Dr.

          To Wages A/c

❖ For Receivable/Outstanding Income : (E.g. Interest)

      Receivable interest A/c   Dr.

          To Interest A/c

❖ For Income Received In Advance : (E.g. Rent)

      Rent A/c   Dr.

          To Rent received in advance A/c

6) **Rectification Entries :** " while writing the books of accounts, possibilities of mistakes in recording the transactions cannot be ruled out. In order to rectify such kind of mistakes, journal entry is to be passed which is known as rectification entry." **For, E.g. Bad debts recovered Rs. 1,200 were wrongly credited to the account of Tarak Mehta, who paid amount.**

      Tarak Mehta A/c   Dr.   **1,200**

          To Bad debts recovered A/c   **1,200**

............xxxxxxxxx............

www.ingramcontent.com/pod-product-compliance
Lightning Source LLC
Chambersburg PA
CBHW080836180526
45168CB00006B/2705